A Rag, A Stomp & A Reel

Sequentially Arranged American Fiddle Tunes for Cello Solo or Duet

by Renata Bratt

To access the online audio go to:
WWW.MELBAY.COM/30793MEB

WWW.MELBAY.COM

Introduction

This book is arranged in sequential learning order – from first position with simple rhythms through fifth position with syncopated rhythm. Some tunes in first position can be quite challenging due to quick string crossings and syncopated rhythms. Each tune has an accompanying cello part, for playing with your teacher or a cello buddy. If you have a friend who plays the guitar or another chording instrument, they can accompany you using the chords written over the staff.

At the top of each tune you will find the key. Feel free to play through the scale that goes with the tune before you start to practice the tune itself. There are also a couple of sentences with information about the difficulty level of each tune. This includes which strings to use, which positions you should use to play it, and other pertinent details.

You will see various descriptions of tunes. A **breakdown**, **reel** or **hoedown** is a tune with two beats per measure – usually in cut-time. A **waltz** is a tune with three beats per measure. A **country rag** is also played with two beats to a measure, often has at least three sections and is very chromatic. A **stomp** is a tune with two beats per measure featuring rag-like syncopation and chromaticism. **Old-time** has become synonymous with fiddle music from the Southern USA.

I have been collecting fiddle tunes that are fun to play on the cello for the past twenty years or so. I teach many different types of cello students – adults and children, who play all sorts of styles. I often supplement a teaching point from another cello method with a fiddle tune that has the same information in it, for example playing in second position, playing music on three strings with extensions, slurs in different combinations and syncopated rhythms.

Most of the accents in this book (as well as for fiddle tunes in general) are produced by yanking the bow a bit. Use more bow rather than pressing down on the stick to make your accent. As with all fiddle tunes, the bowings in this book are NOT meant to be the only ones possible. These slurs and accents are my own personal preferences at this time. You can redo them at any time. Folks who play fiddle tunes rarely play the same bowing twice – that's part of the fun of playing a tune a bunch of times in a row (which is what fiddlers do when they get together). Also, I have included the chords (letter names) over the tune to make it easy to create your own chord accompaniment. The accompaniment can certainly be varied any time.

I have included a few tunes that can also be sung. It's fun to sing as well as play a tune – particularly with a group of friends. Singing is a great way to learn a tune and will help you play more in tune and with better rhythm. The more that you sing, the easier it becomes. You can even sing and accompany yourself!

I learned many of these tunes and songs from my friends, the fiddlers Darol Anger, Matt Brown and Bruce Molsky. I encourage you to purchase their versions of these tunes as well as listen to them on your favorite media platform. You can also attend a summer fiddle camp and learn to play lots of tunes by ear with other players.

Renata Bratt

Contents

Barlow Knife

Key of G Major

Old-time hoedown

In first position. Uses A, D and G strings (mostly D and G). Two slurs.

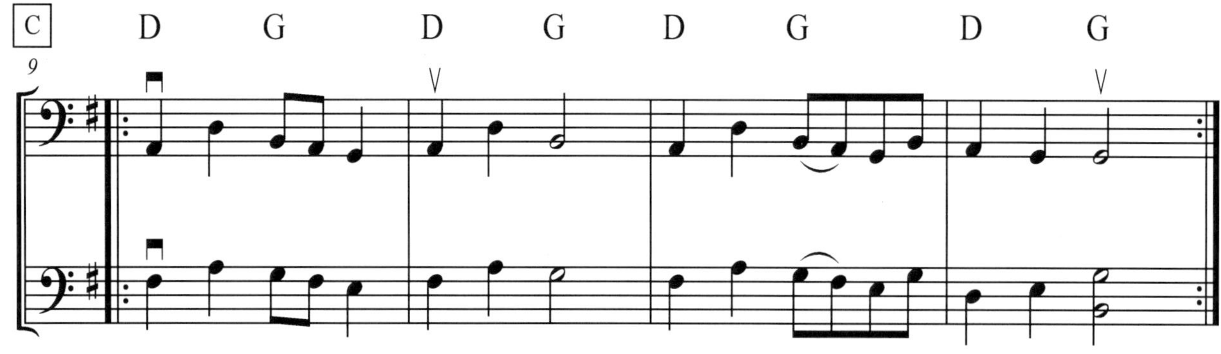

Cotton-Eyed Joe

Key of D Major

Traditional folk song

Uses first position on the A, D and G strings. Bow lift and set. Optional Fiddle Break with slurs.

Verse

D A D

Tune

Eigh - teen, nine-teen twen - ty years a - go, Daddy knew a man named Cot-ton Eyed Joe.

Made a fid - dle ma - de him a bow, made a lit - tle tune called Cot-ton Eyed Joe.

Accomp.

Chorus

5 D A D

Where did you come from where did you go? Where did you come from Cot-ton Eyed Joe?

Fiddle Break (Optional)

9 D A D

13 D A D

You may play the Fiddle Break after each chorus if you'd like. You may end with the Fiddle Break or after the Chorus. The form is up to you!

Green Grows the Laurel

Key of G Major

American/Celtic folk song

Uses first position on A, D and G strings with some syncopation and a few slurs.

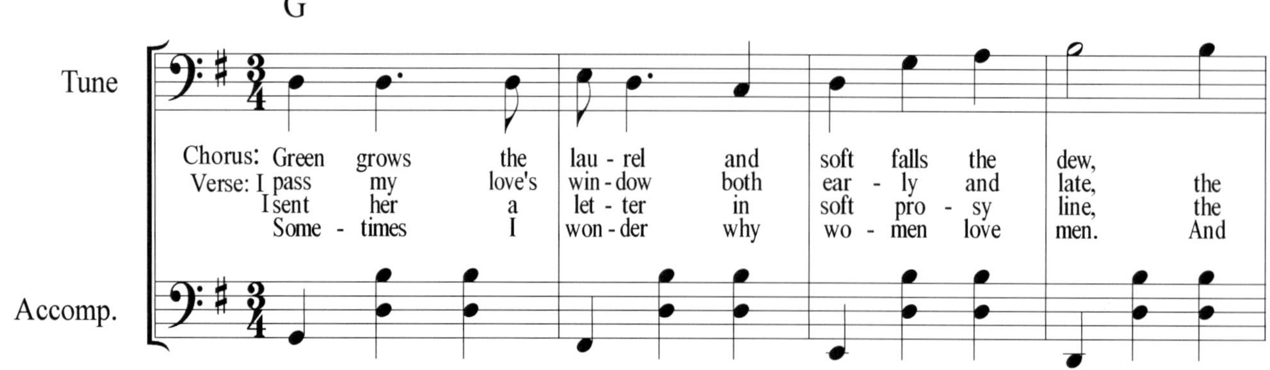

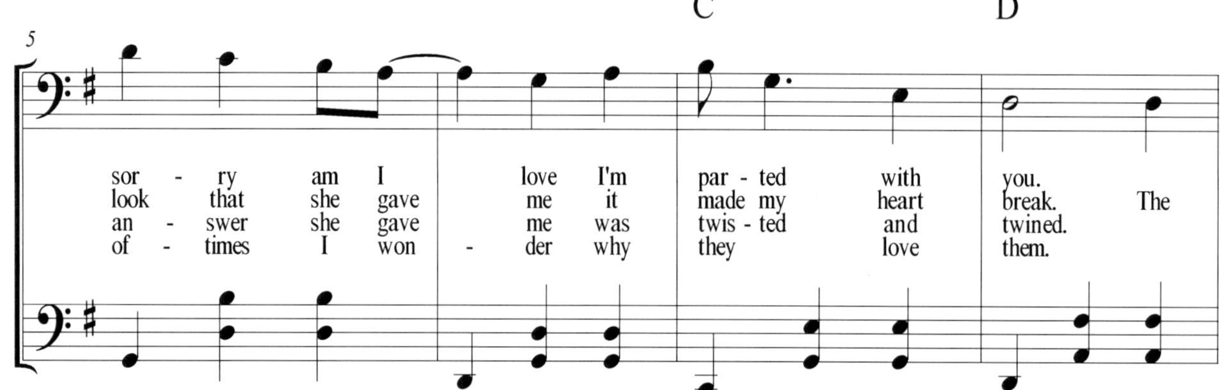

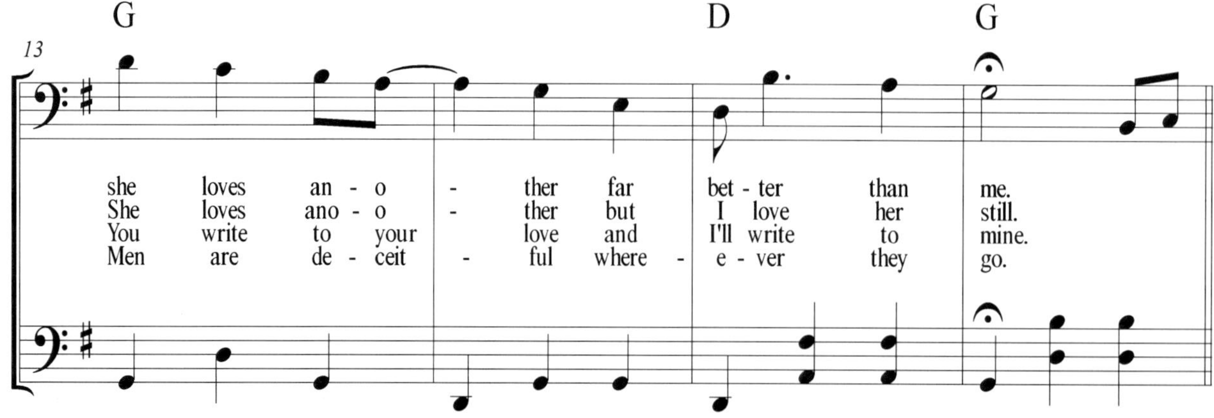

You may alternate the chorus with the verse, if you decide to sing. You may add the Instrumental Break on this page at the end of each verse, each chorus, or every time. Use the fermata only to end the tune. You can end with the fermata at measure 16 or measure 32. The form is up to you! On the recording, I play the Tune, Instrumental Break, and Tune again (Chorus, Break, Verse One).

Ducks on the Millpond

Key of D Major

Old-time breakdown

In first position on A, D and G string with syncopated rhythm and slurs.

The accents above should be played by yanking the bow quickly. Use more bow instead of pressing down. These slurs may be difficult at first. They make the tune sound more syncopated. If you are having problems with any slurs or bowings, don't do them at first. You can add the bowings in after you become more familiar with the tune. Play with separate bows or make up your own bowings. Playing fiddle tunes should be fun!

Sail Away Ladies

Key of C Major

Traditional folk song

Uses first position on A, D and G strings with some syncopation.

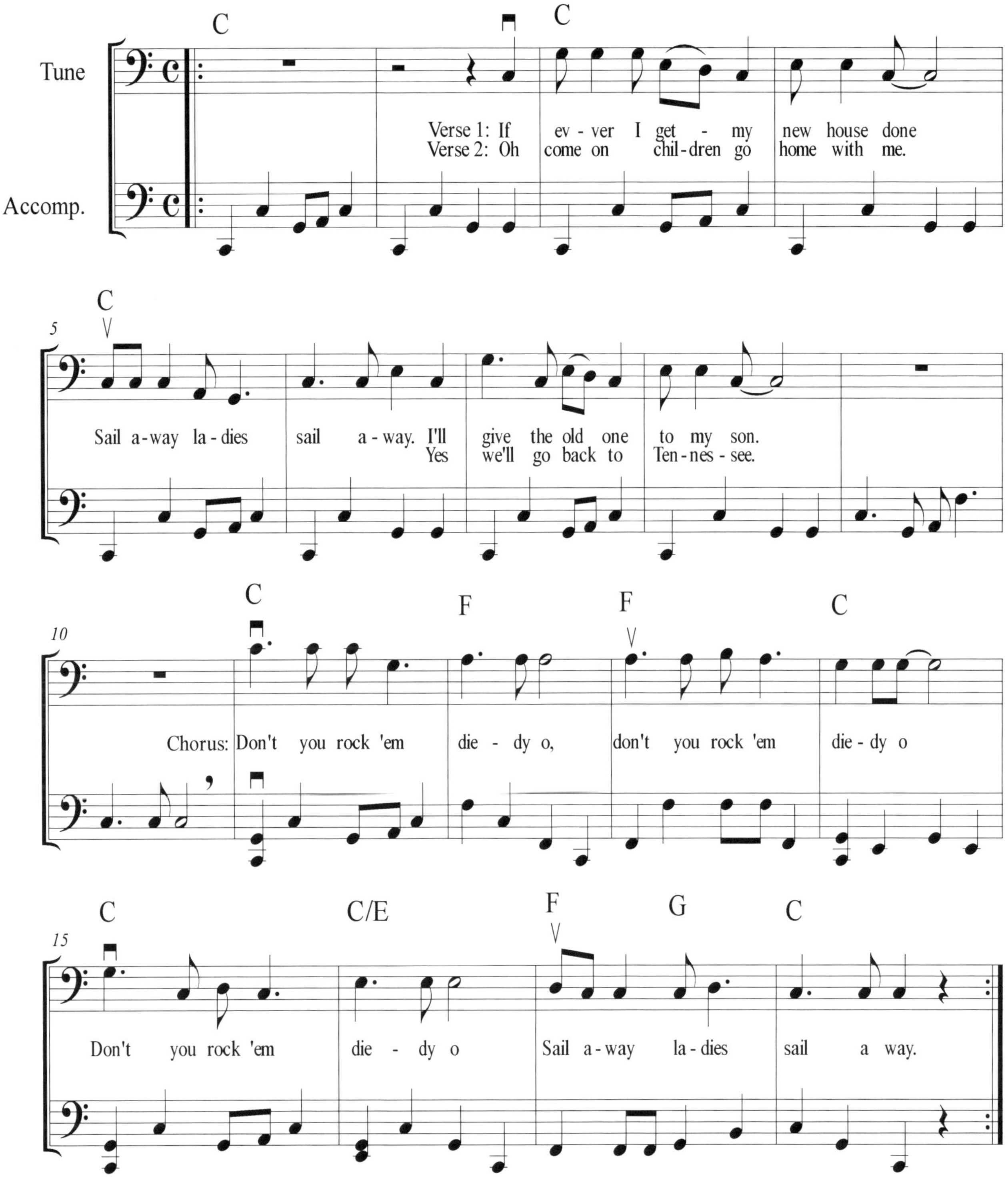

Tune

Accomp.

Verse 1: If ever I get my new house done
Verse 2: Oh come on children go home with me.

Sail away ladies sail away. I'll give the old one to my son.
Yes we'll go back to Tennessee.

Chorus: Don't you rock 'em die-dy o, don't you rock 'em die-dy o

Don't you rock 'em die-dy o Sail away ladies sail away.

If you decide to sing, you may alternate singing the verse with playing the verse. You can play the chorus or the verse as an instrumental break if you would like. As always, the form is up to you!

Lazy John

Key of D Major

Traditional folk song

In first position on A, D and G strings with some syncopation.

Swing!

Tune

Accomp.

A D A D A D A D

Verse: Work-in' all the week in the noon day sun, fif - teen cents when Sa - tur-day comes. Go - in' to a dance to have some fun why don't you get a-way La - zy John?

Go - in' to a dance on Sa - tur-day night ain't coming home 'til bald day light. Then I'm go-na take my girl back home; why don't you get a-way La - ay John?

D G A A D G A A D

Chorus: La - zy John, la - zy John; why don't you get your day's work all done? I'm in the shade and you're in the sun; why don't you get a-way La - zy John?

If you decide to sing, you might like to start playing from the Chorus at measure 9 as an introduction (and to find your pitch).You can also alternate singing the verse and playing the verse. You can play the chorus or the verse as an instrumental break if you would like. Let the other musicians in your band know, the form is up to you!

Over the Waterfall

Key of D Major

Old-time breakdown

In first position on A, D and G strings. Uses syncopated rhythm and slurs with a bow lift and set.

Cluckin' Hen

Key of D Major

Old-time breakdown

In first position using A and D strings. Syncopated slurs across strings and bars. Left hand pizzicato.

+ indicates Left Hand pizzicato

A D

Tune

Accomp.

5 pizz. arco 1. 2.

B D G D D A D

14 D G D D G 1. A D 2. A D

The accents above should be played by yanking the bow quickly. They are speed accents. Use more bow instead of pressing down.

You can use the middle or index finger on your left hand to pluck the A and D strings in the A and C sections. Try both out and see which one feels better for you.

Oh Shenandoah

Key of D Major

American folk song

In first position on A, D and G strings. Bowing with long bows and slurs.

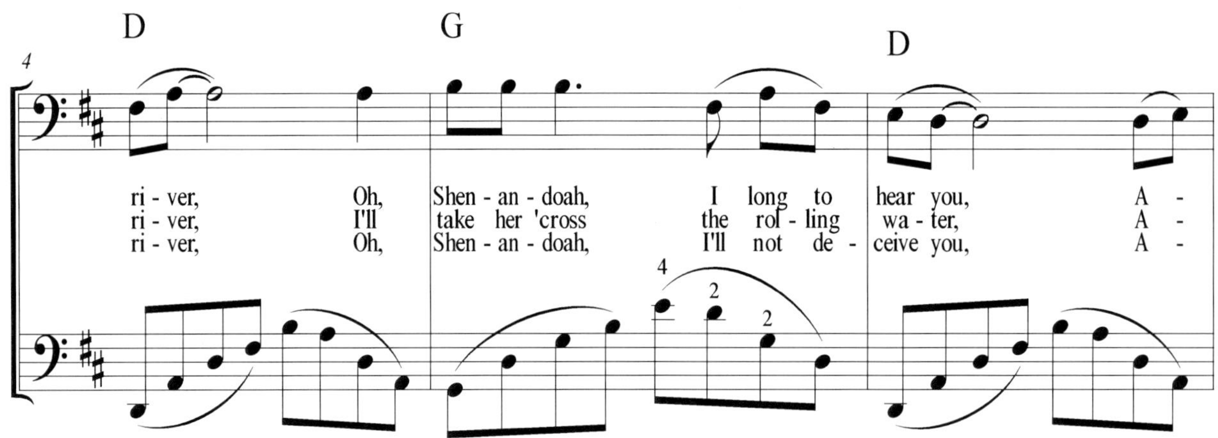

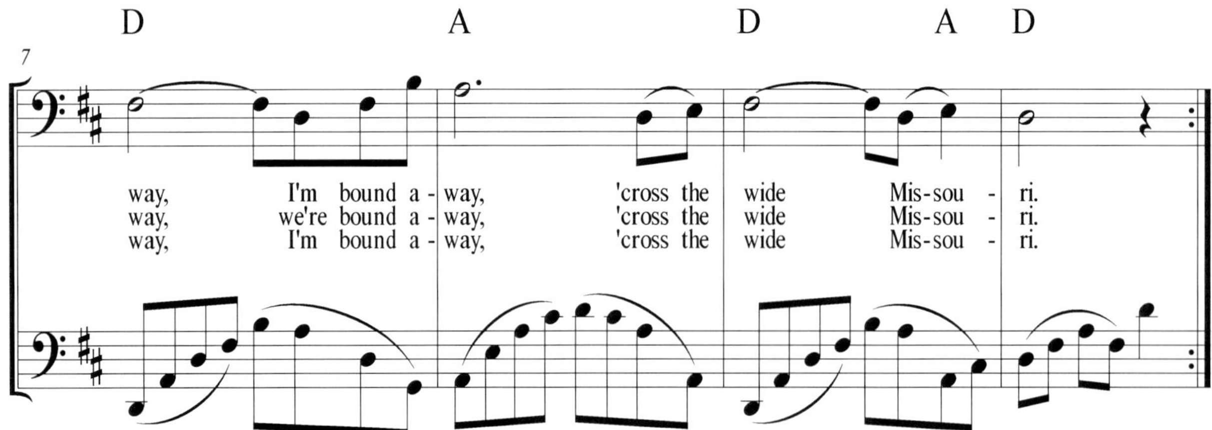

If you decide to sing, you may alternate singing the verse and playing the verse. Play any phrase as an instrumental break if you like. You choose.

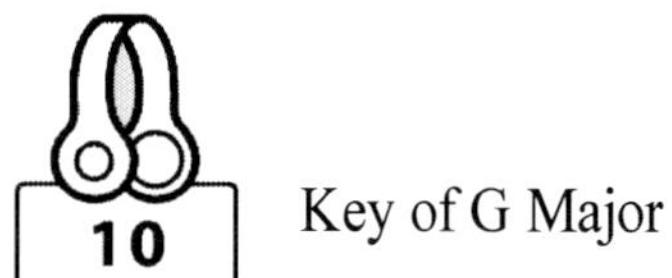

Ora Lee

Key of G Major

Old-time breakdown

In first position on A, D and G strings. Uses accents within slurs, double stops and syncopation.

Not Fast A G G Amin D C D

Tune

Accomp.

5 G Amin D 1 G 2 G

B 10 Bmin G Emin Emin C Amin

15 D D Amin 1 G 2. To A G 2. To end G

The accents above are speed accents. Use more bow instead of pressing down. If you decide to repeat the whole tune (always repeat both the A and the B sections), take the second ending at measure 18. If you want to play the tune only one time, or any time that you want to stop, take the ending measure 19.

Duck River

Key of D Major

Old-time breakdown

In first position using A, D and G strings with slurs and syncopation.

A

Not Fast

Tune

Accomp.

D G A

D G 1. A D 2. A D

B

D G A

D G A D

The accents above are speed accents. Use more bow instead of pressing down.

Leather Britches

Also known as *Lord MacDonald's Reel*

Key of G Major

American/Celtic reel

In first position using A, D and G strings. Some syncopation and slurs.

A G D G

Tune

Accomp.

5 G C D D G

B 9 G D G G

14 G 1.C D G 2. G D G

The accents above are speed accents. Use more bow instead of pressing down.

Devil in the Strawstack

Key of G Minor Pentatonic

Old-time reel

First position using A, D and G strings with 2nd finger. Slurs and syncopated with fast string crossings.

A

Gmin Gmin F Gmin Dmin

Tune

Accomp.

Gmin Gmin F Gmin Dmin Gmin

B

Gmin F F Dmin

Gmin F Dmin Gmin

Use speed accents instead of pressed accents.

Cumberland Gap

Key of G Major

Old-time reel

In first position using all 4 strings with syncopated rhythm and bowing.

A

G C C G D G

Tune

Accomp.

5

G C C G D G

B

9

G C C D G

13

G C C D G

The accents above are speed accents, not pressed accents.

Seneca Square Dance

Key of G Major | Also known as *Waiting for the Federals.* | Old-time reel

In first position. Uses A, D and G strings with double stops, cross bowing and syncopated rhythm.

A
G C
Tune
Accomp.

G D 1. G 2. G

B
G C

G D 1. G 2. back to beginning G 2. ending G

If you decide to repeat the whole tune (always repeat both the A and the B sections), take the second ending at measure 18, If you want to play the tune only one time, or any time that you want to stop, take the ending measure 19. For the accents above, use speed accents instead of pressed accents.

Billy in the Lowground

Key of C Major

American/Celtic reel

In first position using all four strings. Featuring slurs with quick string crossings.

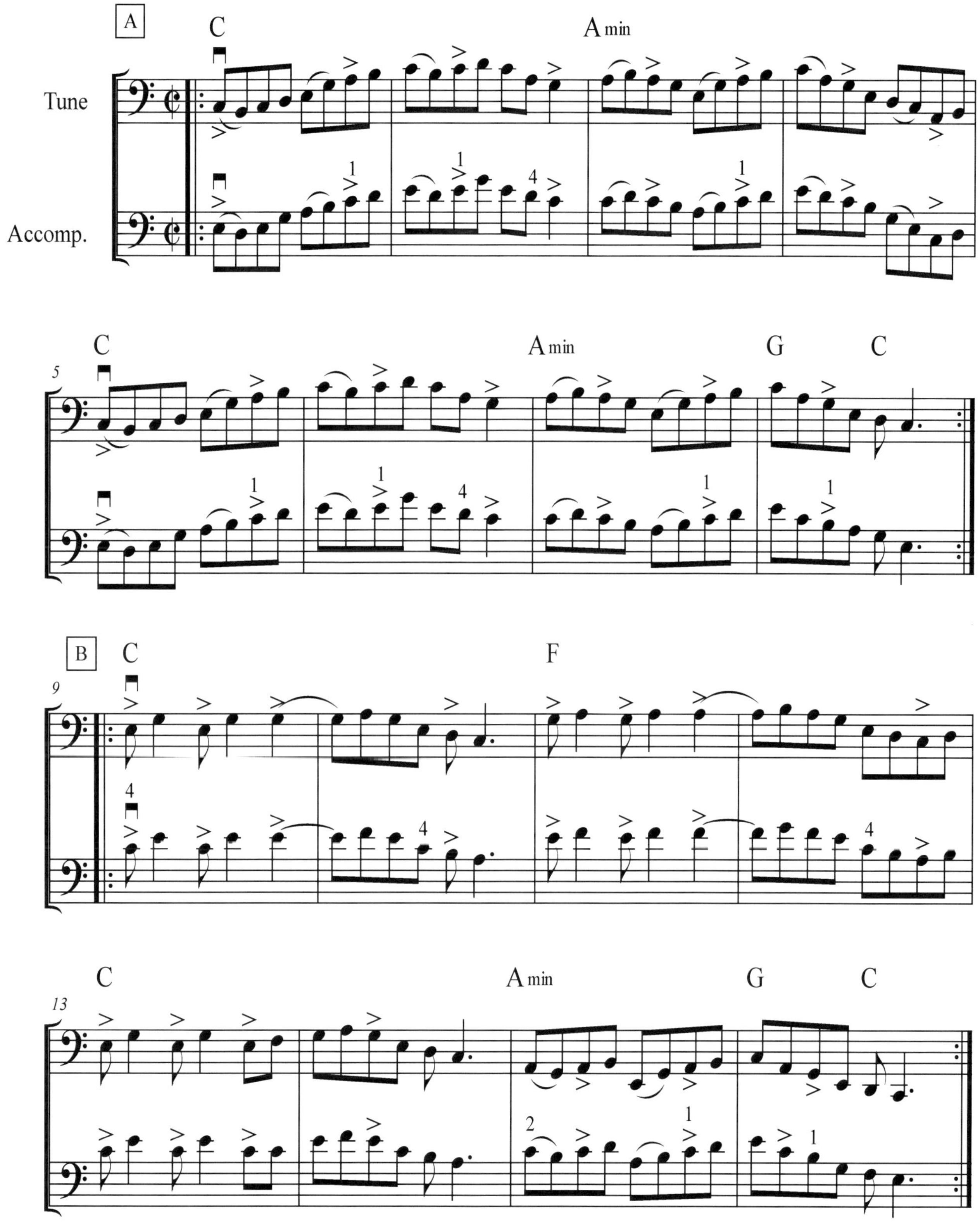

A C Amin
Tune
Accomp.

C Amin G C

B C F

C Amin G C

Use short bow strokes if you want to go fast. All accents above are speed accents, not pressed accents.

Sally Johnson

Key of G Major

Bluegrass breakdown

In first postion. Uses A, D, G and C Strings with fast string crossings, syncopated fiddle style slurs and accents.

A

G C G G Em

Tune

Accomp.

G C C♯dim D 1.D G 2.D G

5

B

G G Em D Em

pizz.

G G C D G

14

Use speed accents for the accents above.

Shove the Pig's Foot a Little Further into the Fire*

Key of G Major

Appalachian breakdown

In first position. Uses A, D and G strings. Fast string crossings and very syncopated with slurs and double stops.

* A "Pig's Foot" is a blacksmith's tool.

Use speed accents for the accents above.

Dry and Dusty

Key of D Major

Old-time breakdown

In first position using all four strings. Features forward extension on G and C strings with double stops and accented slurs.

* An x indicates that the first finger is one whole-step away from the second finger. As always, there is a half-step between the second & third and the third & fourth fingers.

The accents above are speed accents. Use more bow instead of pressing down.

Lost Girl

Key of G Major

Old-time breakdown

Uses A, D, G and C Strings in first position with forward extension and double stops.

Use speed accents instead of pressed accents.

Georgia Railroad

Key of A Major

Old-time breakdown

In first position with forward extension.The A section uses A and D strings only. The B section uses all four strings and remains in extended position throughout.

* An x indicates that the first finger is one whole-step away from the second finger. As always, there is a half-step between the second & third and the third & fourth fingers.

Use speed accents, not pressed accents.

The Road to California

Key of D Major

New England reel

In first position with forward extension. Uses A, D and G strings with fast string crossings, slurs and double stops.

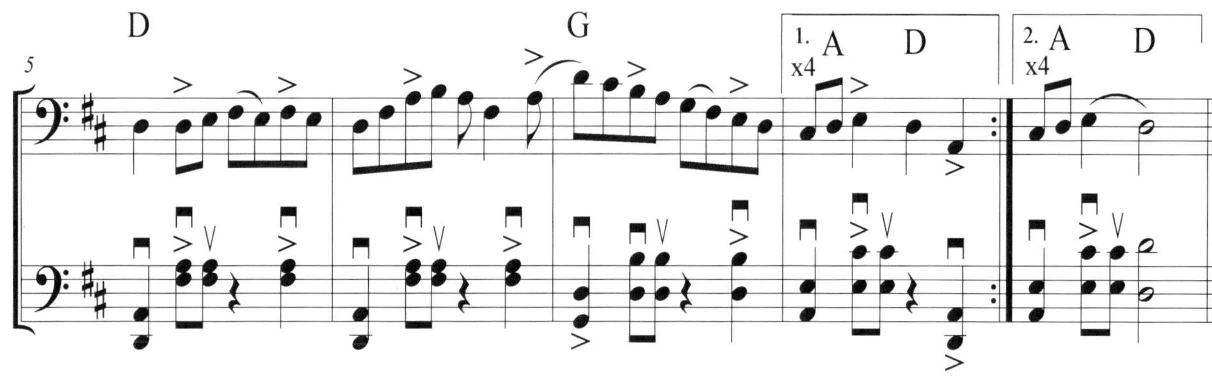

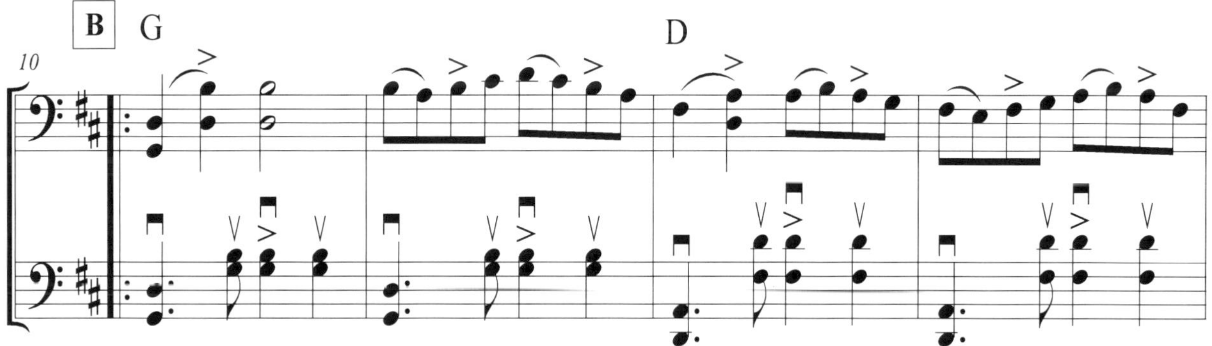

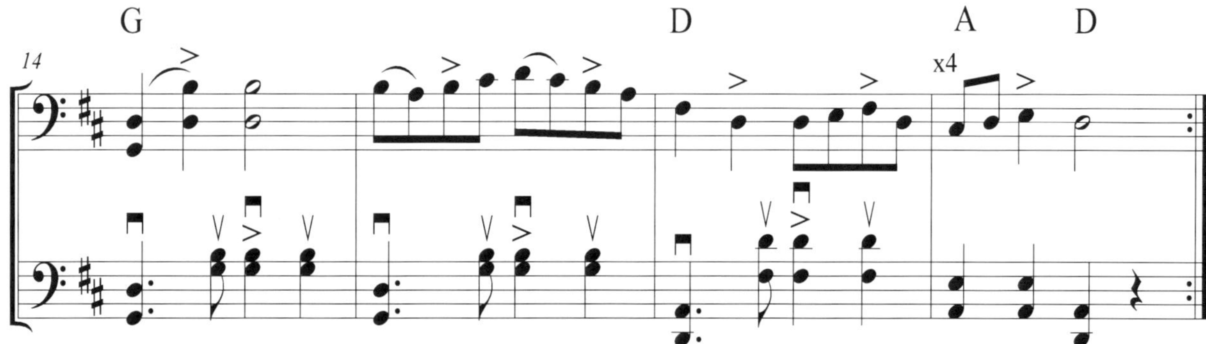

The accents above are speed accents.

Garfield's Blackberry Blossom

Key of G Mixolydian | Appalachian breakdown

In first position on all four string strings, with forward extension on the G string and half position on the C string. Features double stops, fast string-crossing, syncopated rhythm and yank accents.

A G

Tune

Accomp.

5

1/2 pos.

9

13

1/2 pos.

The seventh note in the Mixolydian scale is a lowered 7th. In the key of G Major, the seventh note would be F sharp, but in the key of G Mixolydian, the note is F natural. This version of Garfield's Blackberry Blossom also features a G scale with a raised fouth (the C sharp) throughout. All of the written accents are performed as speed accents. Use less bow for all of the notes if you want to play faster.

Lady of the Lake

Key of A mixolydian

Appalachian breakdown

First position with forward extension work. Uses A, D and G string with accents and syncopated slurs.

*In measures 1-2 and 5-6 some musicians play a "D" chord. That's pretty spicy - try it out with your duet partner.

** An x indicates that the first finger is one whole-step away from the second finger. As always, there is a half-step between the second & third and the third & fourth fingers.

Too Young to Marry

Key of D Major

Old-time breakdown

Mostly first position with forward extension and three notes in second position. Uses A, D and G strings.

Tune

Accomp.

pizz.

second pos.

The accents above are speed accents. Use more bow instead of pressing down.

Saturday Night Waltz

Key of G Major

Old-time country waltz

First and second position on A, D and G strings with many double stops.

swing eighths

A

G C D

Tune

Accomp.

6 C G C

13 D G B G 2 4 2 C 2 4

second pos.

20 2 1 D G G 2 4 2

second pos.

27 C 2 4 2 1 D G 2 1 2

Willow Creek

Key of G

Old-time breakdown

Uses A, D and G strings with first position, back extension, and second position. Features highly syncopated rhythmic bowing and accents.

Tune

Accomp.

A

B

2nd pos.

1. and 2. to return to A

2. To end.

If you decide to repeat the whole tune (always repeat both the A and the B sections), take the first ending at measure 16, If you want to play the tune only one time, or any time that you want to stop, take the end measure 17. Use speed accents, not pressed accents.

Back Up and Push *

Also known as *Creole Belle* by Jens Bodewait Lampe c. 1900

Country rag

Key of F Major*

Uses A, D and G strings in first and second position. Features open string unison with second position back extension in the A section and very fast string crossing in the B section.

* Often played in C - ask your fiddle playing buddies to play this tune down one string!

** An x indicates that the first finger is one whole-step away from the second finger. As always, there is a half-step between the second & third and the third & fourth fingers.

At measure 33 use the fermata only if you decide to end the tune. Otherwise, repeat back to A and keep on playing in time. Use speed accents, not pressed accents.

Beaumont Rag*

Key of F Major*

Country rag

Uses backwards extention first position and extended second position. Lots of chromatic "blue notes" with syncopated rhythm are combined with fast string crossings.

A

Tune

Accomp.

C7 F

2nd pos. (extended)

C7 F

C7 F

2nd pos. (extended)

B♭ B dim F D7 G7 C7 F

2nd pos. (extended)

*Some folks play this in D. Call out your key (F) before you play this in a group. Use speed accents where accents are marked.

** An x indicates that the first finger is one whole-step away from the second finger. As always, there is a half-step between the second & third and the third & fourth fingers.

Forked Deer

Key of D Major

Old-time breakdown

Uses A, D and G strings. First position, extended first position and second position. Features bowing with accents and syncopated slurs.

* An x indicates that the first finger is one whole-step away from the second finger. As always, there is a half-step between the second & third and the third & fourth fingers.

Use speed accents where notated. Use less bow for the eighth-notes if you want to play faster.

Blackberry Blossom

Key of G Major

Bluegrass breakdown

Uses A, D, G and C strings with first, second and third position (forward extension) on D string.

Tune

Accomp.

A

G D7 C G C G A7 D7

1 x2 1 2 1 3

3rd. pos. 2nd pos.

5

G D7 C G C G 1. D7 G 2. D7 G

1 x2 1 2 1 3

3rd. pos. 2nd pos.

B

10

E min B7 E min

15

1. C G D7 G 2. C G D7 G

Use speed accents where written. Play lightly and with less bow if you want to go fast.

Black Mountain Rag*

Key of D Major

Country rag

Uses A, D, G and C Strings. In first, second and third positions with added open string double stops, slides and some chromaticism.

*This tune is often played in A Major. Let your friends know your key before you start. Use speed accents where notated.

C
D
G
4 1 3
1
3rd. pos.
21
D
A
x4
2
x1
D
D
G
x4
3
1
x2
1
2nd pos. (extended)
pizz.
29
D
A
D
x4

Paddy on the Handcar

Key of G Mixolydian

Old-time breakdown

Uses A, D, G and C strings. Extended first position and third position with fast string crossing, rhythmic syncopation as well as bowed syncopation.

Tune

Accomp.

A G F F x4 G

Yank!

5 G x4 3 D 1G 2G

B

10 G F

Yank!

14 G 1 3 G D 1 1 G 2G

3rd pos.

Where notated, use speed accents, not pressed accents.

June Apple

Key of A Mixolydian. Old-time reel

Uses A, D and G strings. With forward extension in 1st position. 2nd and extended 3rd positions.

Use speed accents where notated. Play lightly and with less bow if you want to go fast.

Chinquapin Hunting

Key of D Major

Old-time reel

On the A, D and G strings. In first and third position with forward and backward extension.

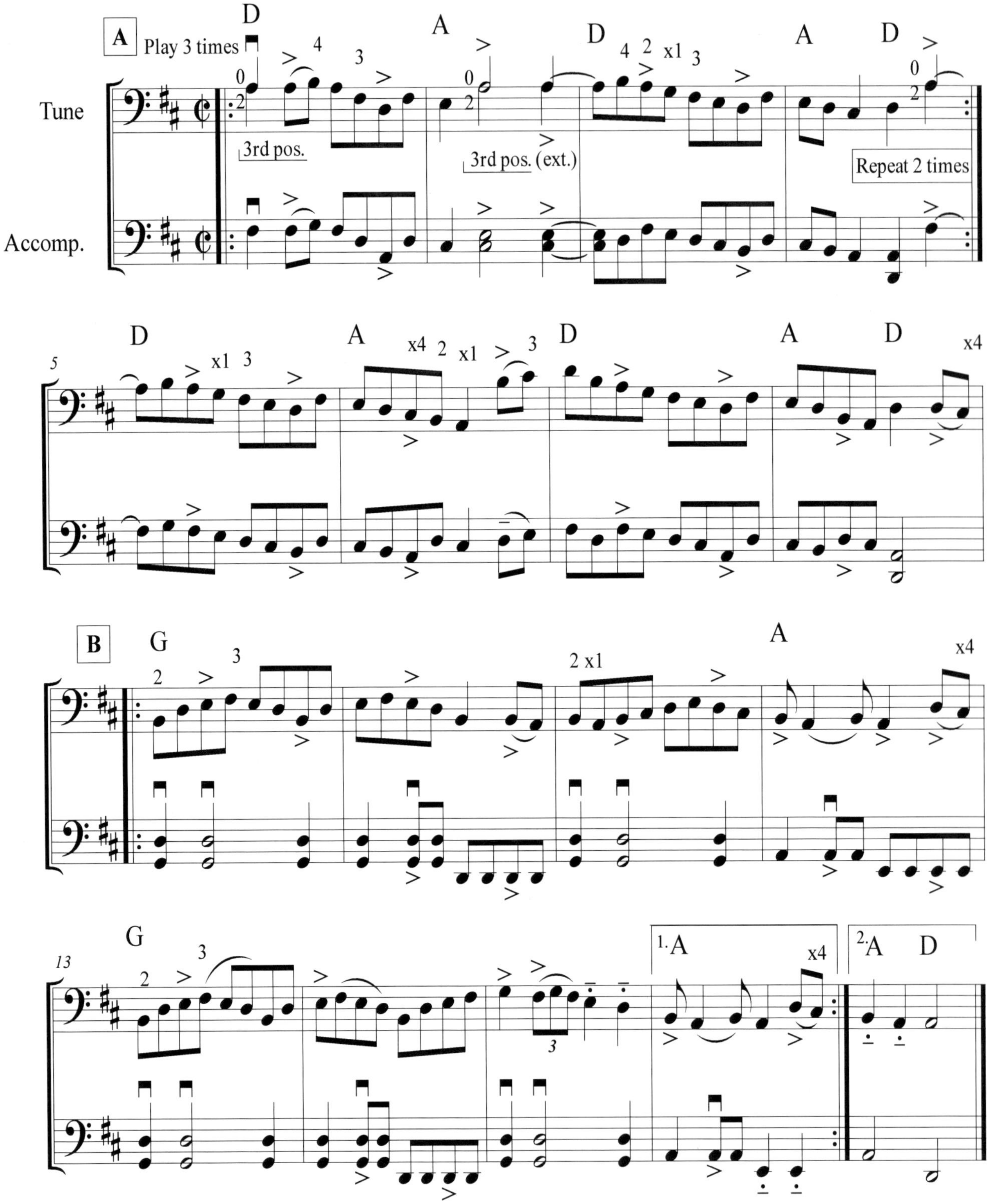

A Play 3 times

Tune

Accomp.

3rd pos.

3rd pos. (ext.)

Repeat 2 times

B

There should always be 16 measures in the A section. Make sure that you always play the first four measures three times. Use speed accents where notated.

The Girl I Left Behind Me

Key of G Major

American/British/Celtic march

On A and D strings with first and fourth positions only.

Tune

Accomp.

A

B

4th pos.

G C G G D

Susanna Gal

Key of D Major

Old-time breakdown

On A, D and G strings in first, second, third and fourth positions, highly syncopated with extension and double stops.

Tune

Accomp.

A D A D 3rd pos.(ext.) 4th pos. 3rd pos. pizz.

D A 1. D 2 D 3rd pos. 2nd pos. 3rd pos.

B D G D A

D G A 1. D 2 D 2nd pos. 2nd pos.

All of the notated accents are speed accents.

Salt Creek

In A Mixolydian

Old-time/Bluegrass breakdown

Uses A, D and G strings. With first, second and fourth position and double stops.

All of the accents above are speed accents. Do not press the bow.

Westphalia Waltz

Key of G Major

American/Polish country waltz

Uses A and D strings. With first, second , third and fourth position featuring vibrato and full bow.

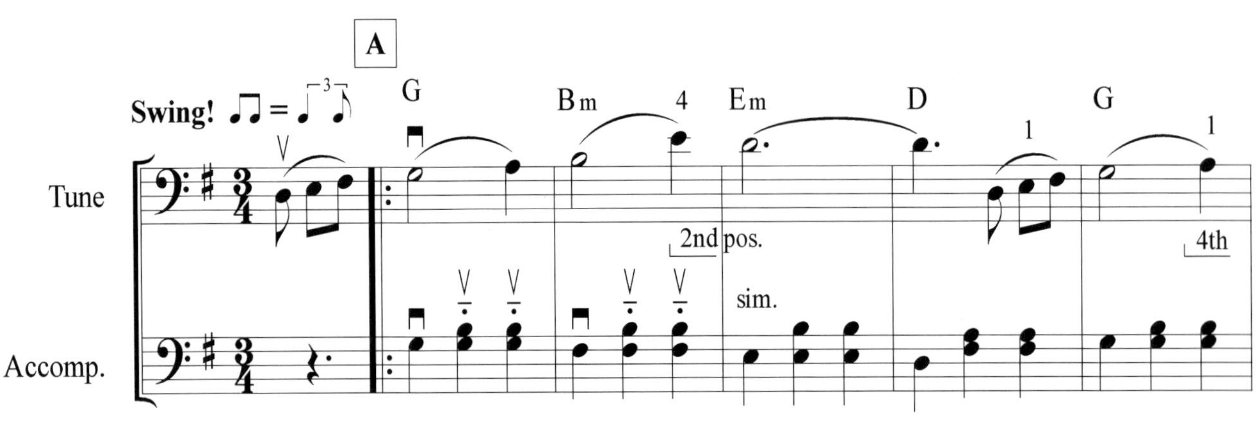

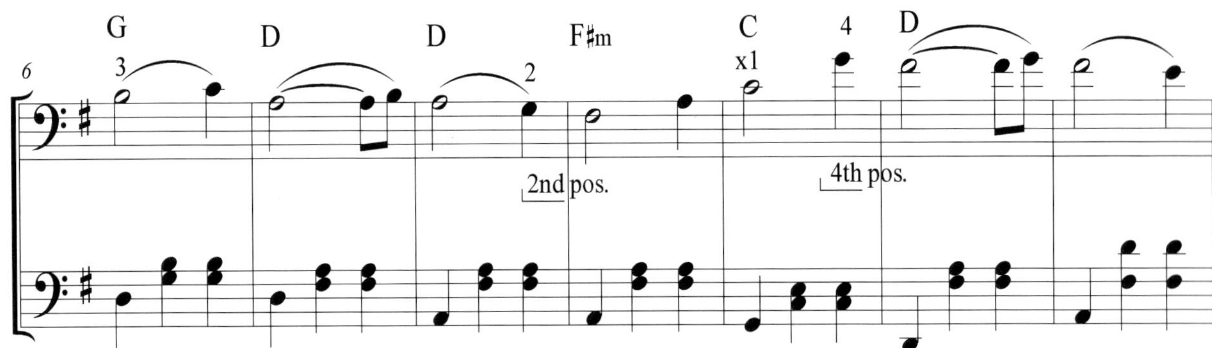

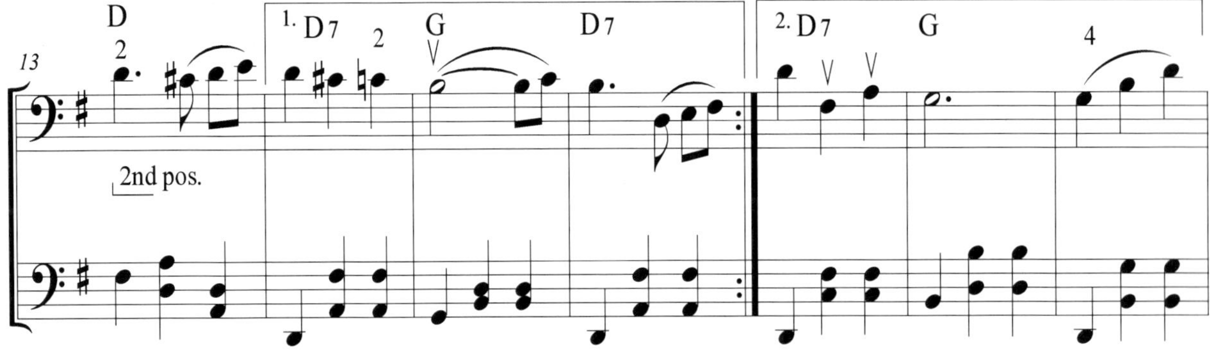

Country style waltzes are often played with a slower vibrato on the longer notes and a rich, full tone. That's why it's good to play with a fingered A (measures 7 and 8) rather than on the open string A.

B
G
Bm
C
G
G
Em
Am
4th
3rd pos.
4th
D7
Am
C
D
4th pos.
2nd pos.
1. D7
G
D7
4th
2. D7
G

Ragtime Annie

Key of D Major

Old-time breakdown

Uses A, D, G and C strings. In first, extended first, second and fourth position. Features arpeggios, syncopated-style bowing and fast string crossing.

A
D
D
A7
Tune
Accomp.
A7
5
1
1.4D
2.4D
B
D
Em
A7
14
x4
x4 2 x1 0
D
3
1
4 1 2
2nd pos.

Use speed accents where notated.

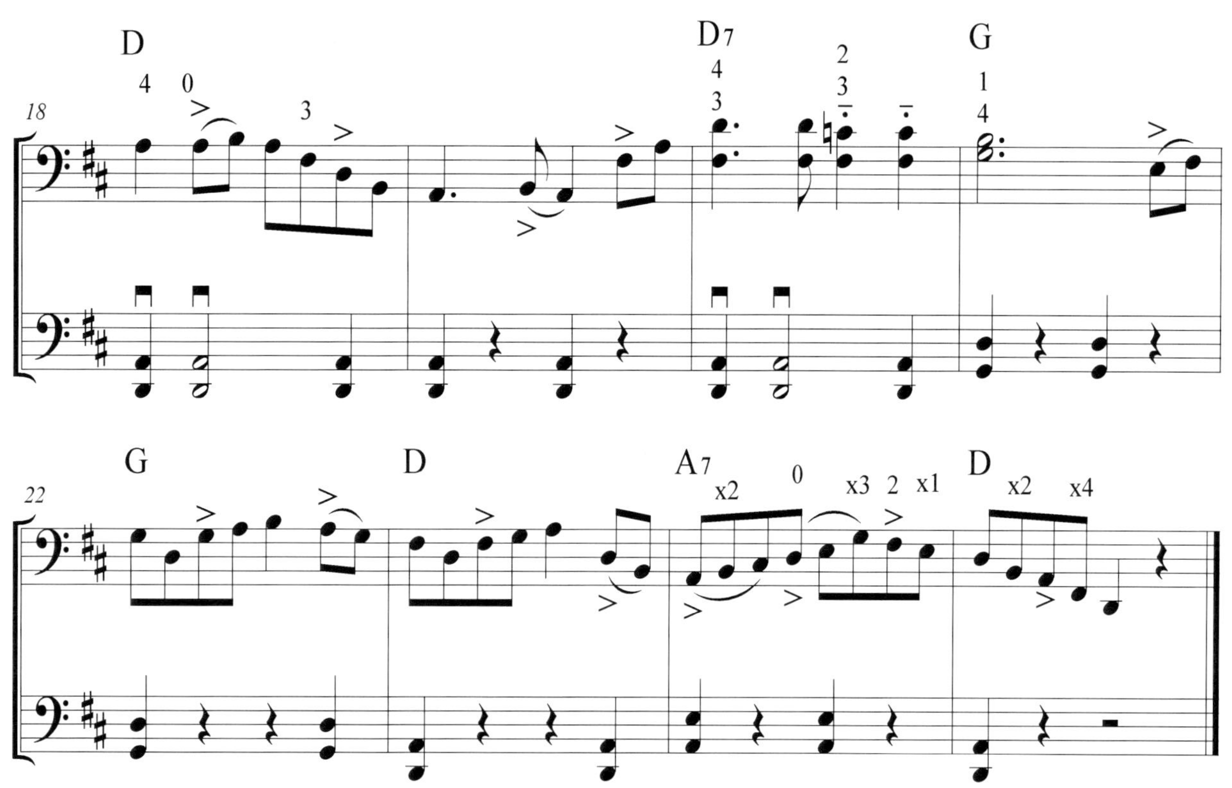
D
D7
G
G
D
A7
D

Carroll County Blues

Key of G Mixolydian

Old-time country rag

On A, D and G strings. With first, third (closed and extended) and fourth positions and slides. Very chromatic notes and syncopated rhythm.

Swing!

Not Fast

A

G

Tune

Accomp.

4th pos.

3rd pos.

4th pos.

3rd pos.

4th pos.

3rd pos.

pizz.

C

G

3rd pos.

4th pos.

Experiment with slides in this tune. Slide with your fourth finger into the F natural at measures 1 and 3. Slide with your first finger into the B natural at measure 5 and into the E natural at measure 7 and 8. Try placing accents on different notes. For instance, in measure 1, you could accent the first beat and the F natural. Or you could accent the first D and the Bb. You could accent the beginnings of of slurs or the note that they slur into. Part of the fun of playing fiddle tunes is changing up the slurs and the accents.

13
2.
x3
4
x1
x3
2
1
x4
D
4
4
4th
17
2
B
G
3
2
21

Soldier's Joy

Key of D Major

American/Celtic reel

Uses A, D and G strings. In first, third and fourth position with extensions, arpeggios, syncopated bowing and fast string crossing.

Use speed accents where notated. Play lightly and with less bow if you want to go fast.

Temperance Reel

Key of G Major

American/Celtic reel

Uses A, D and G strings. First, second and fourth positions as well as the A octave harmonic with strong bowed fiddle shuffle pattern.

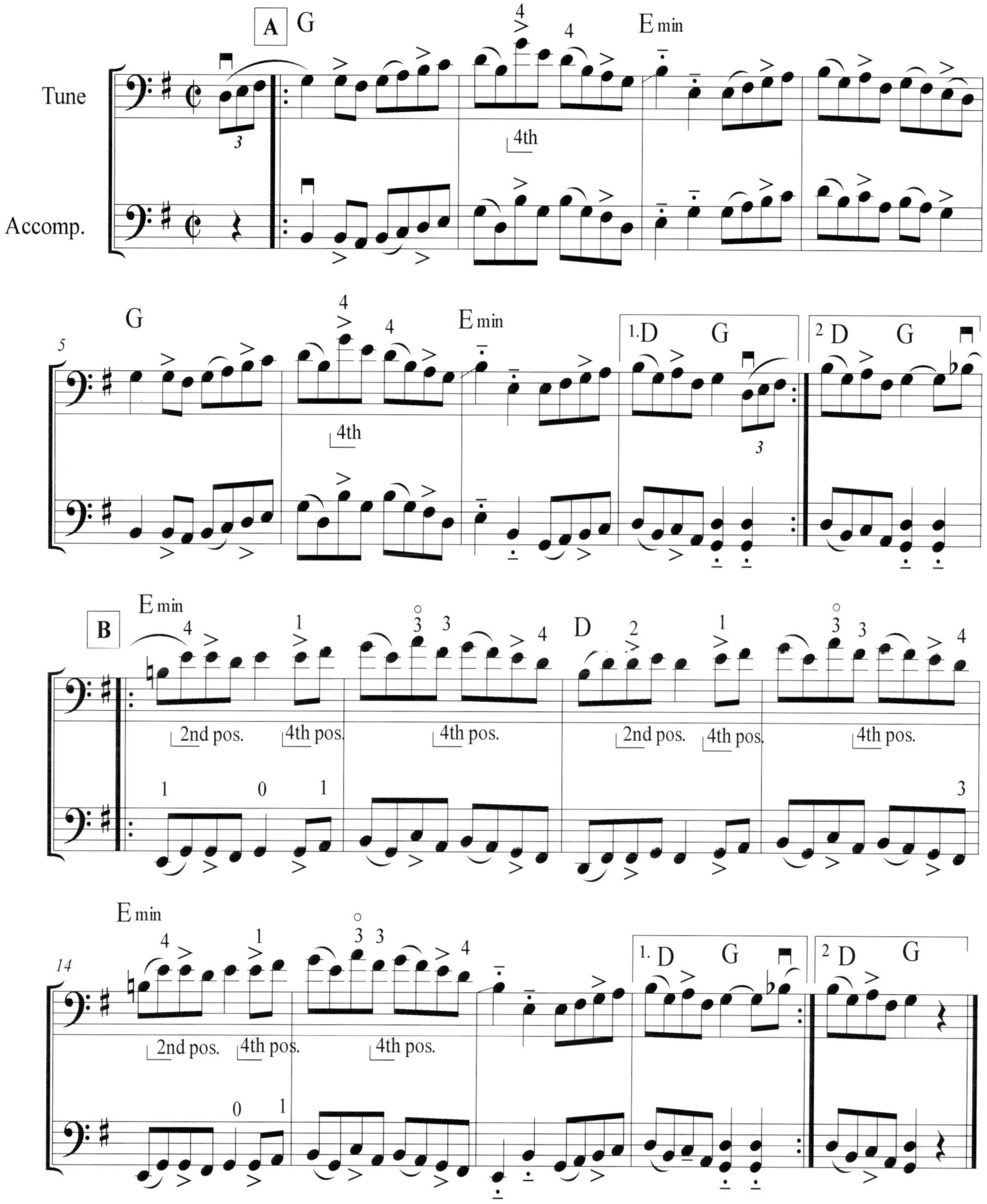

Tune

Accomp.

A G 4 4 E min 4th

5 G 4 4 E min 4th 1. D G 2. D G

B E min 4 1 3 3 4 D 2 1 3 3 4

2nd pos. 4th pos. 4th pos. 2nd pos. 4th pos. 4th pos.

1 0 1 3

14 E min 4 1 3 3 4 1. D G 2. D G

2nd pos. 4th pos. 4th pos.

0 1

Use speed accents where notated. Play lightly and with less bow if you want to go fast.

Acorn Stomp

Key of F Major

Old-time country rag

Uses A D, and G strings. In first position, extended second position, third position, fourth position and fifth position.

Create your own speed accents for this tune. Change the bowings if you like. Fiddle tunes are rarely played the same way twice.